SOCIAL MEDIA

Dominating Strategies For Social Media Marketing with Twitter, Facebook, YouTube and Instagram

Introduction

I want to thank you and congratulate you for downloading the book, *"Social Media : Dominating Strategies for Social Media Marketing with Twitter, Facebook, Youtube and Instagram."*

This book contains proven steps and strategies on how to create and grow a strong social media brand presence so that you can tap into the limitless potential that social media has to offer.

Every business owner or marketing executive now agrees to the fact that their business has to adapt to social media or end up losing touch with its customers. If the report by eMarketer is anything to go by, the over 1.73 billion people who are on social media cannot be overlooked; one in every four people uses social media today. From a marketing perspective, we all know that is a hell lot of market for us to tap and penetrate with greater efficiency and effectiveness. It doesn't matter whether you are a small or large business; you can use social media to target your target audience, interact with them and widen your customer base beyond levels you could ever imagine.

Knowing that there is a huge market isn't enough; in any case, everyone knows that! You need to know how to build your social media presence so that you can derive the full benefits. How do you do that and how do you ensure that you keep on succeeding in each one of your strategies? This book will introduce you to the world of social media to help you appreciate the importance of using various tips and strategies when marketing your business on different social media platforms.

Thanks again for downloading this book, I hope you enjoy it!

Table of Contents

Social Media: Adapt Or Die

Gone are the days when small businesses could not advertise their products to the masses because of cost restrictions, as large corporations that have huge marketing budgets scramble for all TV and radio ad space!

So, what do you do to fully use social media to derive the most benefits? As a rule of thumb, don't just get right into it without proper planning. You need to figure out how you are going to execute your plan in a manner that guarantees success. Here is what to do before you jump right into social media marketing and end up making some costly mistakes. But before we go there, what do you understand by the word "social media?" Well, much as it seems like an obvious word that you would know, you probably don't have any specific definition of what it is. Nevertheless, it refers to applications and websites that make it possible for users to create and share different kinds of content or take active part in social networking. In simple terms, these are platforms that enable the user to participate in the communication process (at least you should know that the internet is nothing more than just an information database that we all try to access). With social media, you can add comments, add videos, like or 'participate' in any other form. It includes social bookmarking, social news, wikis, social networking and social photo and video sharing just to mention a few. Therefore, the journey to building a strong social media brand entails having a strong positive presence in as many of these forms of social media as possible. If you are still wondering why you should really embrace social media or die, here is why:

Why go social?

Increased brand recognition

Think of different social media sites as a street intersection that attracts different numbers of people at different times and your presence in the different platforms as your billboard at that intersection. The more pronounced or outstanding your billboard is, the more the number of people who are going to notice who you are. Just like the billboard, having strong social media presence will help boost your brand recognition since as we have seen, 1 in every four people uses social media. Social media provides an avenue for your brand to be seen and heard while making it easy for your current and prospective customers to find you. For instance, someone will know about your company by simply seeing a friend's recent activity of liking your page. Additionally, someone could be wowed by your photos on Pinterest making them gain some interest in your business. Your social media updates also help you rank highly in the search engines especially because they are indexed a lot faster. This in turn means more people can find you with a lot of ease. The more your brand becomes visible on social media and the more you engage your target audience, the more your business grows.

Increased opportunities to convert

Think of every new post you make on social media as a prime time ad. This simply means that you have an opportunity to sell (even if it isn't hard/direct selling) to your audience, which in turn means that there will be some conversions. Unlike in a TV or radio ad where those who are not actively watching or listening don't get to see your ad, the fact that the post is written or in picture format means that current, past and future followers/customers will have access to such content, which simply means that the conversions will be perpetual. With every post, video, comment or image, you are presenting an opportunity for your audience to react in the form of a visit to your website, email subscription, or purchase or any other form of conversion that you have set. Although every post won't result to a positive conversion, the more you interact with your following, the more chances you have that someone will want to react. The fact that you are giving your audience an opportunity to react is enough to attract attention.

Reduced marketing costs

Most small businesses cannot compete with large multinationals that have huge marketing budgets for advertising space on TV and radio. This means TV and radio advertising are out of the question as far as advertising is concerned. The internet and in particular the social media has made it a lot easier and less costly for small businesses to target their audience with great ease. You could even reach out to over 10,000 highly targeted people with a budget of less than $20 if you are opting for paid advertising. This is a very tiny fraction of how much it would cost you to advertise on TV and radio. Nonetheless, if you don't want to go this route, spending about 6 hours a week is enough to result to increased traffic; you can split this into one hour daily for 6 days.

Enhanced customer insights

You can easily listen to what people are saying about you, about themselves and about different issues that concern them that might be of interest to you. By following people's comments, likes, shares and follows, you can easily tell what it is they really like. This can in turn help you make an informed decision with respect to the kind of content to share, when to share it and how to share it. You can then try different campaigns just to help you understand what works and what doesn't.

Enhanced brand loyalty

A research published by the Texas Tech University has proven that by engaging your current, past and prospective customers through social media, you are likely to enhance brand loyalty. This could be mainly because people want to be heard and answered whenever they have anything that they need answers on. Actually, another research published by Convince & Convert showed that over 50% of Americans actually follow the brands they are loyal to on social media! As you can clearly see, you have everything to gain when you engage your audience through social media.

Better customer experiences

Engagement could be taken as interacting with your friend; as you well know, the more you interact with anyone, the more you get to know them and the closer you become. The inverse is true; if you don't interact, you will grow apart! Social media is a communication tool that allows direct communication between you and your current and prospective customers. Unlike phones where you answer questions to individuals, with social media, you are interacting with your followers live, which simply means that other people could easily check out older threads if they are looking for something.

The more you engage your customers, the greater their level of satisfaction, which as we all know is one of the top ingredients to nurturing customer loyalty. Social media can help you clear confusion and misunderstandings making it easier to keep customers happy. For instance, if a customer complains about your product or service on Facebook, it is easy to address that issue publicly either through offering an apology or explaining whatever issue is bringing confusion. It doesn't have to be complaints; you can also appreciate a follower's positive comments just to show that you really appreciate that feedback.

Improved brand authority

Have you noticed that people always tend to brag about their experiences on social media? When more people are talking about great experiences they have had when using your products or services, you definitely stand to gain if you have a good social media presence. Actually, as people talk about you, new users regard the brand highly. This ultimately results to more conversions and easier attainment of your company's objectives.

Tap SEO power

If you have any experience in marketing a business online, I know you are aware of how hard it can be to appear in the top search results of the different search engines. Actually, updating a blog as often as possible, having excellent meta descriptions and having backlinks isn't just enough to make you get a spot in the top searches for your targeted keywords. The truth is that search engines nowadays largely consider social media presence in determining the rankings of different sites. Therefore, the more presence you have on social media, the higher you are likely to rank in the search engines since you are considered trustworthy, legitimate, and credible. It is pretty simple, right!

Greater inbound traffic

Before using social media, the only people who will probably visit your website will be those who are already familiar with your brand and those who are currently searching for the keywords that you rank highly (if you have any). When you create a new social media profile, you are actually building a new avenue for people to visit your website and check out what you have on offer. This coupled with the fact that every post is an opportunity to attract interest means that you are actually increasing the number of ways through which people can see you, which ultimately results to increased conversions.

With the countless ways in which you stand to gain when you embrace social media, I know that you are definitely interested in getting started right away.

Getting Started

Well, before you get started in social media branding, you need to do some form of preparation to be sure that you know where you are headed to; in any case, how can you tell where you are headed when you don't have a plan? Answer the following questions to get started:

*What is your objective for social media utilization?

*Who is your target group?

*What is your expectation out of that particular social media site?

*What is the easiest way of attaining your objective?

So, why do you need to answer these questions? Let's understand how each of them relates to attaining your ultimate goal of succeeding in developing your social media brand.

#Setting objectives

Your objectives for using social media could be such things like:

*Developing awareness about your business

*Engaging your target audience effectively and building customer loyalty

*Increasing website traffic in a bid to increase leads

*Increase the credibility of your business to become a thought leader

*Increase conversions/revenue generation

*Enhance operational efficiency

*Spur innovation through observing and sharing trends

As a rule of thumb, ensure that your objectives or goals are SMART (Specific, Measurable, Attainable, Relevant/result focused and Time-bound). Obviously, these need to be detailed enough to ensure that you don't leave anything to chance. Let's talk about this in greater detail:

Specific

Ensure everything is simple and clearly defined in order to eliminate fuzziness in all your goals. In simple terms, you get rid of all ambiguity when you make your goals specific. Don't just say that you want to be more social or want to make more sales with social media; instead, you should specify what "more" means to you. Just to help you get started as you develop any social media goal you should ask yourself some very important questions:

*What do you really want to achieve with your actions?

*Who is really involved with the goal?

*Where exactly is your activity located?

*Why do you really want to achieve the goals you have set?

*When do you want to start working towards the goal and when do you want to accomplish that?

*What exactly is needed to get the job done?

Let me give you an example:

By February 1st, I want to have attracted 100 likes to my Facebook page by posting 2-3 times a day and responding to customer queries within 24 hours.

Just to help you understand, this answers when the goal is to be achieved, specifies the goal (100 likes) and how to get it done.

Measurable

Your specific goals should have a measurable milestone such that you can tell how good or bad you are doing based on the set targets. For instance, you can measure your posts in terms of the number of people that specific post has reached. This simply means that the method of measuring performance in different social media sites is bound to be a lot different. For instance, you could think of such things like number of shares, number of retweets, likes, follows, reads etc. You can also measure it in terms of the number of people who actually purchased your product or service due to your social media activity. Here is an example just to make you understand what I am talking about:

By April 1st, I will have increased my content sharing, clicking and commenting by 10% to help us reach a larger audience.

The example above is pretty straight forward and features specific measurement criteria of a 10% increase in comments, shares and clicks, which will be the indicators of an increased audience and engagement.

Achievable

We all know that any goal you set should be challenging such that it pushes you to move out of your comfort zone. However, it shouldn't be unachievable or frustrating to achieve. As such, you should first evaluate your current skills level and resources before you can set the goals. Test your skills level before setting the goals just to be sure that you can actually achieve such goals.

Relevant/result focused

You must measure goals and not your social media activities. For instance, you shouldn't set goals such as sending 20 tweets daily. Instead, you should focus on what these actions are meant to achieve; this could be increasing awareness of your brand and many other subtle goals. Here is an example to help you understand what I am talking about:

By May 1st, I will develop a system that directly ties all social media activity to lead collection through giving a sign up reason for an exclusive newsletter where I will be delivering early-bird deals to customers.

As you can notice from the above example, the result here is to achieve a 1-1 contact with customers.

Time bound

You don't have until eternity to do what you have to do to achieve your social media goals. Your social media marketing goals should be properly timed to create a sense of urgency and tension that pushes you to achieve your goals. All the examples I have mentioned already had a date if you were keen to notice!

When you have everything thought out as far as goal setting/ setting of objectives is concerned, you also have to consider the target audience for your marketing efforts.

The target audience group

Determine the target audience for your social media marketing efforts; you simply cannot be targeting everyone! Unlike in TV and radio advertising where you might not have the options on who to target, social media has such options so you need to choose who you target. You can make a decision based on:

*Age group

*A particular community

*Gender

*A particular group that has interest on specific products

*A global presence

*A particular location

*People who have certain preferences

*Those using a certain social media platform

It will become very easy to choose any social media platform if you settle on the target audience. The next step is to map your expectations from whatever social media site you will settle on. In any case, any SMART goal should be Specific, measurable, attainable, relevant and time bound.

What is your expectation from using any social media platform?

As you list your expectations, you should ensure that you are very specific about what you want. That is the only way you can tell whether you are actually attaining your objectives or not. Different social media platforms also have different conversion rates so you have to understand that beforehand so that you can know what to expect from your marketing efforts. Here are some things to answer before you can continue:

*What level of performance do you want to attain?

*How easy is it to attain that level of performance?

*What will you need to attain that level of performance?

*How many people do you want to attract in the process?

*Will you be able to measure your audience Vs increase in sales with precision?

Once you map out your expectations, the next thing you need to do is to determine the best strategies to use to attain your objectives and expectations with ease.

What is the easiest way of attaining your objective?

Every social media site has its "hacks" that the pros have already mastered so that you can attain faster results. You need to understand what is needed for you to attain that. Do you need to pay anything in the process or is it something you can do on your own? Do you have to get any technical expertise for you to attain your objectives with greater ease? When you answer these pertinent questions, you will be well on your way to developing a strong social media brand.

After deciding on that, the next step is to start evaluating the different social media platforms so that you can tell how they will be of importance to you in developing a social media brand. You will discover that you might probably need many of the social media sites/ applications discussed in the next segment once you read how to use them and the benefits you can get from using such applications. We will look at each individually and in detail to help you understand how to develop a social media brand in that site/application/platform so that you can unleash the full power of that particular platform.

Tips On How To Dominate Facebook

Facebook boasts of over 1 billion active monthly users spread across the globe making it by far the most popular social media site across all age groups and societies. Facebook also attracts over 4.5 billion likes daily, 665 million active users daily, and over 765 million mobile monthly users. With this huge user base, it means that you can take advantage of the platform to promote your business to Facebook's users. Going back to our billboard analogy, Facebook is the busy intersection where over 1 billion people pass through so having some presence there will mean that you can attract a fraction of this insanely huge number. Just to give you some inspiration on why using Facebook is critical, let me give you some reasons why:

Why use Facebook?

In addition to the social media marketing benefits we've already talked about, these are pretty much unique to Facebook.

The numbers

As I already mentioned, Facebook is by far the biggest social media site based on the number of users. In Facebook, the secret is to get as many people as possible to see your posts or your brand, like it, follow, share or whatever action they have to take. The good thing about Facebook is that it is used virtually everywhere around the world so you can be certain that there will be millions of people in whichever location you are in. The fact that an average Facebook user spends about 21 minutes daily means that being on Facebook and sharing your content gives you an opportunity to engage with as many people as possible. Well, here is an interesting fact that will give you greater motivation. An average Facebook user has about 130 friends. This simply means that when you share anything that people share, you are creating a ripple effect when several people share that. Your posts could easily go viral if they can generate many shares because whenever anyone shares anything, such people are subtly promoting you. As such, the key to success is ensuring that your posts capture the attention of the first group of people who encounter that content so that you can stimulate response.

Cross promotion

Facebook is constantly updating its algorithm such that people see less of irrelevant content on their feeds. One way of ensuring that you get people to see your posts is to have a Facebook Fan page for your business. This Facebook page acts like some sort of mini website for your business. Although this doesn't automatically mean that the numbers will jump from one hundred to tens of thousands of users, you can be sure that the more you keep promoting the business, the more it grows and the more it promotes your website or brick and mortar store. We will talk about how to move from few likes to thousands or tens of thousands of likes later in the book.

Future proof

As I already mentioned, Facebook is always updating its search algorithm. For instance, recently, Facebook banned the use of like gating as a method of attracting likes (we will discuss this later). Paying for advertising seems to be a norm today unlike in the past where it was easier to promote a business without paying a cent. Although this (paid advertising) is fairly easy and affordable, it is better to use the method now and not later because as more businesses adopt this model, the competition becomes higher, which means that the effectiveness of such ads will probably be lowered. As such, it is better to adapt whatever strategy you use to get likes now and not later! Facebook will definitely not strip you off your likes if you obtained them legitimately even if it updates its search algorithm to make it harder to attract new likes. So, when you have more likes, you are sort of shielded from any changes that might make it harder for you to succeed in future. This also means that you have to invest in providing value to your current audience if you really want to keep them checking your page.

Targeting

Unlike in Google and other search engines where you can only target someone based on his or her search preferences, Facebook allows you to target your audience (if you use paid search) with great precision. For instance, you can target audience in terms of gender, age, location, apps, mobile device use, education, life events, interests, travel, likes and purchase behavior with utmost precision, which simply means that there will be a high conversion rate. This is simply because Facebook users unknowingly or knowingly build a very comprehensive profile about themselves making it a lot easier to target them with pinpoint precision. No other platform, online or offline provides such targeting precision.

If you are using paid advertising on Facebook, you could easily target audience that has similar characteristics as your existing audience, which simply means that the conversions will definitely be higher if your existing audience has had good success. You could for instance target lookalike websites, lookalike pages, lookalike mobile app users, and lots of other lookalikes! This ultimately means greater marketing ease and ease of audience expansion.

I know you know the limitless potential that Facebook provides to your business but what has been preventing you from taking advantage of Facebook to market your business fully is lack of knowledge on how to do it right. In simple terms, you are asking, "How can I effectively market by business or increase my brand visibility through Facebook?"

Here is how:

As we know, Facebook is not only used for chatting; it allows you to upload photos, videos, share the links, share the feelings, and share the interests just to mention a few.

If I am a customer interested in buying a particular product that your business is selling, I will probably first check what others are saying about the product or your business. I will then go on to check reviews, ratings and anything else that would help me make an informed decision on the subject matter.

In that case, if you create a centralized hub for your business in Facebook, don't you think people will find it easier to access all that information in just one place? You can even be answering all questions or concerns that your target audience might be having to make it easier for others to make decisions in future. In simple terms, you might not need to be answering the same questions over and over again when you have a central page on Facebook since people can always read responses relating to various issues that others have had.

Facebook Page

To get started, simply create a Business Facebook Fan page for your business then invite your friends to like your page, join groups that have interests in your products or business, post all your offers in that page and make your customers to visit that page. Well, since it isn't as obvious as it sounds, let me take you through the business page creation process:

Step one:

Visit this <u>page</u> to create a new page (Please note that you can only create a page when you are already a Facebook user so if you don't have an account, please create one. You can use your personal account if you want this account to act as the admin account for that page).

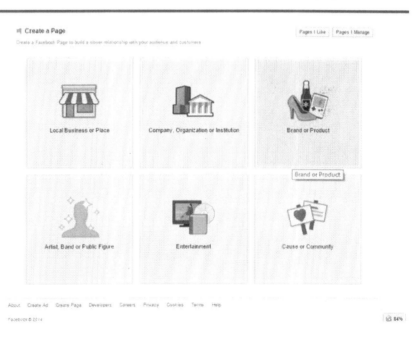

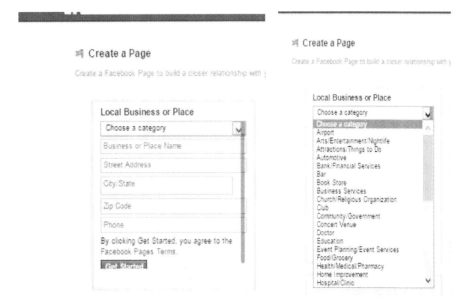

The process is pretty straight forward. However, here are some things to note that will make the difference between a killer page and one that is not:

#Fill all the fields

Make sure you fill everything that needs to be filled including your contact, website (if any), page description, etc. The page description also helps in organic search and Facebook's search so ensure that you use some descriptive keywords just to make it easier for people to find you. However, don't stuff the keywords!

#Categorize your business wisely

This will make it a lot easier for people to search it, which means categorizing your business in the right category can make the difference between being found and being confused with another business. For instance, if you run a bar, don't categorize your business as concert/venue unless you are promoting concert and venues in your bar. Also, don't say it is a food grocery if you are running a plumbing company!

#Customize your page url

You don't want an unprofessional page URL. At best, you should ensure that your URL has the exact name of your page (this helps in organic search in search engines). For instance, if your page is named Greg Orton, your url should be something like *facebook.com/gregorton*. Please note that you can only change your unique address once. Also, you cannot change the Page name when you hit 100 fans.

#Profile photo

The profile picture should speak volumes about your business; you shouldn't just choose anything that comes (It is even advisable to have your company logo).

#Should you start inviting people right away?

I wouldn't recommend that you start inviting people or advertising your page if you don't have anything on your page yet. Your first priority should be to start posting stuff that people would want to check around when they visit your page. Think about it; would you want to like a page that has no photos, updates, likes etc? If you hardly like pages that have nothing to like, don't push people to like your page when it has nothing. Asking people to like a blank page will be a wasted opportunity to sell yourself better.

#So, should you like your page immediately?

Much as you might think that it doesn't hurt to like your page as the first person, I would advise against it. Since liking your page will appear in your timeline, you don't want people to see that you are liking pages that don't have content yet; you want to reserve that for the time you will have populated your page or when you think you have had enough posts to make people to want to share, like etc. In simple terms, liking your page as the first person will be wasting potential traffic, which you should have gotten had you opted to wait until you have populated your page with great content.

#When to invite your friends

If you have guests that you are inviting over to your house, would you want them to find that the house is not in order? Well, if you don't want to be embarrassed by the emptiness in your house, have stuff filled in it; it could be decorative art that captures their attention or furniture! Similarly, your Facebook page needs to have content before you can invite friends to check out what you have been up to!

#Should you pay for ads yet?

Well, much as it might be tempting to boost your posts through paying for ads on Facebook, don't just jump right into it. Instead, you should ensure that you have enough content to keep any lead you generate through paying busy and interested in what you have to offer.

You might think that doing just that will guarantee that you will get the maximum exposure needed for you to have a strong social media brand. This is not the case. You need more than that to succeed; after all, so many others do just that but end up giving up because they don't attain their goals. Do you know why? The reason for all this is pretty simple; they don't get to attract their target audience. Just as in the search engines where SEO is critical for success, you need to use some strategies to succeed in attracting the audience you want. So, how do you attract more likes to your page?

1. Share a link to your Facebook page on the groups that you join-some members of these groups could probably like your page in the process.

2. Add a like us button on your website and share it constantly in your social circles.

3. Invite your business contacts to visit and like your page.

4. Ensure that you have a clear and fresh call to action on your landing page-don't be afraid to ask people to like your Facebook page! You should even set up a landing tab: Before announcing your page publicly, you should probably set this one up; this gives you control to get people to respond to your call to action. Although like gating is not allowed (Facebook stopped this in November 2014), you can use this landing page to increase conversions as opposed to having new people landing on your wall. You just need to set up an effective call to action that will prompt a new visitor to like your page. Even if you don't set up any application, you can pin a post, which has the call to action

5. Use high quality and fascinating images and content to attract people to share your content and even prompt more likes. Actually, you will realize that the more visual you are in your content, the greater the number of likes. Don't be afraid to post video tutorials or share relevant videos on your page to help your audience in various

ways. You can also think of sharing photos of people enjoying your services just to give your business a sense of humanity.

6. Always strive towards telling people what they would want to know about the business or industry; do your research. This means having some information relating to the stuff that happens behind the scenes.

7. Ensure that your email signature has a link to your Facebook fan page.

8. Tag the fan page so that it can appear on your friends news feed. Use the tag @fanpage or #fanpage when referring to your Facebook page. This comes in handy when you have a personal account that already has your friends on it. You could also ask your friends, employees and other groups admins for help on that.

9. Master how to target fans based on their interests, demographics and location.

10. Leverage the existing traffic on your website for greater likes and social media publicity. Place the social media icons near the homepage to maximize click through rate (CTR).

11. Set a specific time when you post and maintain consistency in posting.

12. Use Facebook groups for greater engagement-You can create open, closed or secret groups depending on the nature of discussions that go in this page. We will talk about the power of Facebook groups shortly just to help you realize how much you stand to gain.

13. When everything fails, use paid advertising on Facebook to reach out to your target audience. Well, using paid advertising doesn't mean that you have not had success in what you are doing. This can fast track the entire process thus ensuring that you get more likes within a shorter period without much struggle. Let me discuss this a little further.

The power of a Facebook Ad

A recent survey found that most of the online advertisements are reaching only 27% of their intended audiences. However, the same survey is explaining that an advertisement in Facebook is making 90% reach to its intended audiences. So now you have the understanding about the power of a Facebook advertisement, right? How do you get started?

Though it is easy to think that an ad will result to automatic increase in likes, the real picture is not exactly the same. You need to ensure that you target your ad to the right audience to maximize your conversion rate. Since Facebook paid ads cost money, you don't want to be wasting your advertising credits re-advertising to the same people especially those who have already converted to paid customers. As such, you should master the power of remarketing on Facebook. Let me explain that.

So, what is remarketing?

In its simplest terms, remarketing is simply a tactic that helps you to advertise to individuals who have shown interest in your product or service after visiting your website. In this case, you segment the website visitors through creating custom ads for such groups of people. In this case, only such people get to see such ads on Facebook. In essence, remarketing on Facebook enables you to increase conversions while ensuring that you keep your cost of customer acquisition as low as possible. One of the greatest benefits of this technique is that it only shows ads to those who are genuinely interested in whatever you are selling. For instance, you can remarket to those who already visited your website but did not buy anything or those who have already completed an initial sale. Another target audience for your ad could be those who don't know about your product but are already interested in something similar.

Since there are both organic and paid visitors, you need to ensure that you differentiate paid and organic traffic. So, how do you stand to gain if you start remarketing?

Reduced cost per click

Remarketing on Facebook results to reduced cost per click (much lower than on search engines) especially because Facebook traffic is usually supposed to be far less targeted than any search engine traffic. In essence, people on search engines are already searching for a certain product or service, which means that they are asking for your service. On the other hand, social media traffic is not as targeted because people are not actively looking for whatever you are selling. In the search engines, users are usually searching for a particular product, which means they are asking for your product (pull marketing) but in social media, the users are not really searching for anything and may not even convert to paying customers (push marketing). This in turn makes Facebook ads a lot lower than ads on search engine since technically speaking, users on Facebook are not really searching for your product or service at the moment. Here is a picture showing how to hyper target your audience.

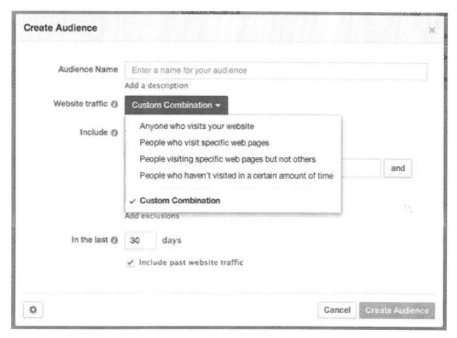

With this model, you can easily target people who have visited your site but have not converted yet, which means that you are ultimately keeping your cost per click costs low while maximizing customer acquisition. To go about this, you will need to have consistent quality marketing, which entails customizing the message such that it includes some additional information to what such customers are already aware of about your product since their last visit to your website. With that, you can expect to see increased CTR (click through rate) than other marketing campaigns while ensuring that you keep customer acquisition costs low than first time visitor conversion costs. You are also likely to have a lot better engagement.

#Improve conversion rate

If you have ever marketed anything, you can be certain that converting first time website visitors into paying customers is not easy and takes time. Actually, if your industry is highly competitive, such visitors are likely to be checking out multiple sites before they can even make a purchase. The truth is that they will compare several sites before they can make the purchase so if they leave your site, some will probably have a problem finding your site in future even if they are interested. As such, you risk losing sales if such people don't finally find their way back. Others could probably have converted had they gotten some motivation from your end. Remarketing comes in handy in such circumstances because when such visitors see your ad especially if it features some more info that they probably didn't know, they are likely to convert to paying customers.

With remarketing technique, you can even opt to exclude those who have already made a sale through creating a custom remarketing segment for those who have already visited your thank-you page; in this case, you can prevent them from seeing that campaign.

#With remarketing, you can capitalize on social proof

As you go on with your marketing efforts, try not to be too limited by the fact that you are only targeting 'qualified' customers. You can show your ads to a wider audience such as those who already bought products or services from you just to ensure that you let the two groups of people interact. You will be amazed by the fact that happy customers will be highly willing to post something encouraging that will make those on the fence want to buy from you. Actually, when someone sees that others have already purchased your product or service, they are likely to feel more comfortable buying from you, which means that they are likely to convert to paying customers. By doing this, you are also enhancing your brand loyalty; you want more loyal customers than just new customers because loyal customers will buy from you with little or no marketing effort i.e. near zero cost of acquisition.

One interesting thing about loyalty is that if you extend your audience to start including your current customers, it is a lot easier to upsell while ensuring that you are more social and more engaging. This is mainly because when any customer sees you on any social media platform, they will probably engage you resulting to more conversions.

With that, you will have a larger audience so that you can start attaining your goals. So, what impact should you expect from your efforts?

The Facebook Impact

Now you have created the page and have implemented the strategies for increasing likes that I mentioned above. What should you expect after that? How do you stand to gain from your marketing efforts?

1. When you frequently post offers of your products in the Facebook page, it will make more visitors and more hits to your page. This will drastically increase your web traffic.

2. When you engage your fans on your Facebook page, they will have better experience, which means that they will probably respond positively about your business. This in turn attracts more likes/fans since people want to associate with good businesses that give customers excellent experiences. The more positive comments and reviews you get, the more business will come your way. Once you start receiving positive reviews from the customers through email, you can publish such reviews in your Facebook page in order to attract many more customers, which will generate more leads for you.

3. When you do post sales or post service follow up, it will increase the number of repeat customers; you will also get referrals through word of mouth.

Every business that is on Facebook and is serious about its social media activities can probably pay for likes, and figure out ways of getting people to like its page. However, some businesses are simply exceptional in the way they do their stuff; they don't just do the minimum! Since each business has its unique strengths as far as social media is concerned, you would probably want to spy on your competition just to be aware of what is happening. Here are some creative ways of spying on your competition on Facebook.

1. Make use of Facebook Pages to watch

Your biggest strength here is the fact that very few businesses are using this feature and the fact that the competitor can never know that you are spying. Instead, they get a message that someone has placed them on the watch list (without specifying who). So, how do you start using this feature?

-When you login to your Facebook page, navigate to the overview section located on the Facebook insights tab then scroll down to add page then select this option (although there is an option for you, you can simply search a specific page to add).

-You can then add all the pages that you would want to watch (you have up to 100 pages to add). Ensure that you add a few pages from industry leaders within your niche just to make sure that you are getting insights on what works for them and what doesn't. You could also know which kinds of posts are popular. To check out how a page you are watching is performing, you simply need to click on the page's name to get all the data.

-Go to the section for posts (in the insights page), then click the option for top posts from all pages that you are following (you will get 5 popular posts from all the pages in your watch list). You can get more info about the posts by clicking on each post just to know the type of engagement in each post (likes, shares, comments etc).

2. Use vital photos from post planner

This is a premium service that goes for about $29 a month and helps you get to know such things like all time popular photos. To get info about any page, you simply need to add its URL to the app. So, how can you use that to your benefit? Simple; you can share it on your page to help drive more likes and comments. Just make sure that it doesn't promote the competitor's business (such things like watermarks or copyrighted images are a no no)!

3. Facebook interest list

This is another excellent way of tracking your competition without them knowing. You can add a page to your interest list even if you haven't liked its page. So, how do you set this up?

Locate the interest option on the left side bar of your page's home page then click add interest. You can then move on to create a list then proceed to search for the page(s) that you want to track/monitor then click next. You will then be given an option to provide a name for your list. I should point out that you should set your privacy setting to 'only me' just to ensure that no one else can access it. If you don't mind having the list public, just provide a very descriptive name for your list. You can then click done.

Once you are done, you can always visit the interest section to check the most popular and most recent posts. Through that, you can be more confident on the kind of posts that spur conversation and action. Actually, you can even track your competitor's actions without visiting their page!

4. Use Simply Measured to get free reports

Simply Measured provides free social media reports for literally all social media platforms including Vine, Twitter, Facebook Google+, LinkedIn etc. All you have to do is share your experience with Simply Measured on any social media site. With this platform, you can actually compare 2 weeks reports against your competition. You could also opt to upgrade to the paid service. The downside of this service is that you can only know whether a post is promoted or not by visiting that page, which can be tedious to follow up!

Knowing what your competition is doing and knowing how to attract likes to your page is a very good thing. However, this might not really cut it when you want to be outstanding. Here are some actionable tips on how to customize your Facebook page to make it a "like magnet".

Tips for greater success on Facebook as far as branding is concerned

#Join as many groups as possible and share links to your page as often as possible. You could even post in the name of the Fan page. If done well i.e. images and captivating content, you could easily make people to click on your page and like the page. This in turn increases traffic to your Fan page.

#Be active-Joining the groups isn't enough; you need to post as often as possible (don't spam though). The more people see links to your site, the more they will be inclined to check it out.

#Organize events: Organize events and invite your friends or members of the groups that you have joined. You could hold events in various groups or on your Facebook page. Also, attend other people's events and post comments about various issues discussed in such groups. You could combine this with doing surveys on various issues relating to your business.

#Piggyback on some hot topics-After Gregory Levey wrote the book titled "shut up I'm talking", his Facebook group has grown from the initial 700 people who had purchased his book to over 6million likes.

Try to use catchy headlines and even go on to reference hot-button issues in order to capture the attention of the masses. Actually, the more people like your page, the more people actually continue liking and the viral effect will be highly likely.

#Your Posts: Posts that have between 100-250 characters have been proven to attract up to 60% more likes, shares, and comments than those outside this limit. Be observant on your post length, just to help you analyze how you can actually derive more value from your Facebook posts. You should probably experiment with different post lengths just to help you determine your ideal post length. Trust me; those seemingly minute things that you would probably overlook actually count. Your posts should be short, engaging and shareable.

#Start using link posts in order to drive people to your site

Facebook now shows a clickable thumbnail when you add a link to a website making it a lot easier to attract people to your site. All you have to do is to enter your site's url then press enter. By doing that, the title of the page, plus description and image in that URL will be visible (you can also choose to customize the text or image if you want).

Tip: Ensure that the image that displays is catchy to make people want to click on it.

#Converse with your audience

You should try asking your audience to share their thoughts or feedback with respect to your products and services. Through that, you can easily get to know what customers are looking for and ways through which you can enhance your business. Once this is done, you should then go on to post content that shows that you really took whatever feedback or suggestions they had into consideration. This should in turn build a strong and loyal customer base because they know that you value their ideas.

#Be the discount/promotions business

Everyone loves free stuff. Offering special deals or perks to your Facebook fans is a great way to keep them visiting your page and website just to hunt for free stuff. This will in turn drive more sales and traffic. Ensure that you have clear call to actions that have links to the most relevant page.

Some interesting ways of enhancing engagement include having clear calls to action and even some redemption details. Also, don't forget to let your audience know about when the promotion ends just to help you create a sense of urgency.

You can blend the discounts and promotions with provision of exclusive information to your fans. You will be amazed by the manner in which this gets people to keep on checking your page just to know what is happening. This is a very handy method of driving loyalty and sales because you make your fans to feel treasured/valued because of having exclusive access to events, contests and news just to mention a few.

#Strive towards being timely

I wouldn't want to visit a page that still has last year's cyber Monday offers appearing as its recent posts when it is Easter the year after. As such, you should ensure that you have posts that depict what is happening at the moment. If it is Valentine's day, your posts should probably be tailored towards resonating with whatever is happening at the moment. You should also be timely in your responses; you wouldn't want to be texting a friend who replies to your message five days later! In essence, you will notice that the faster you respond, the more your fans will engage you and the move visits you will have to your page.

Tip: Try posting sneak peeks of some upcoming product sales some 1 or 2 weeks before major holidays like Cyber Monday, Black Friday, Christmas, New Year, Easter, Valentines etc. You will be amazed by how you will keep your fans "glued" to your page!

#Develop a posting calendar

Although it is sometimes good to go with the flow, planning has a profound effect on your success rate in everything you do. Try to have a calendar showing what you want to be talking about (posting) in each week or month. Through that, you can have enough time to research on what you want to post (don't just post aimlessly). You should also try to find a frequency that works for you. In essence, you should try implementing any strategy you embrace for at least a month before you can switch to another strategy if that doesn't work.

#Master how to schedule your posts

I already mentioned the importance of having a consistent posting schedule. What I didn't tell you is that Facebook now allows you to use a scheduling feature just to make sure that your posts go live at specific times. This will help you cover up for times when you might be busy with something else making it hard for you to post. So, instead of failing to post when your audience is expecting your posts, you can schedule posts by clicking the clock icon located at the lower left hand corner of the page's sharing tool.

Tip: Ensure that you schedule your posts when a large number of your fans are online just to be sure that you will have greater engagement. You can know stats about that when you visit your page insights (within the posts tab).

To manage all your scheduled posts, you simply need to head to the top of your page then choose edit page before choosing Use Activity Log.

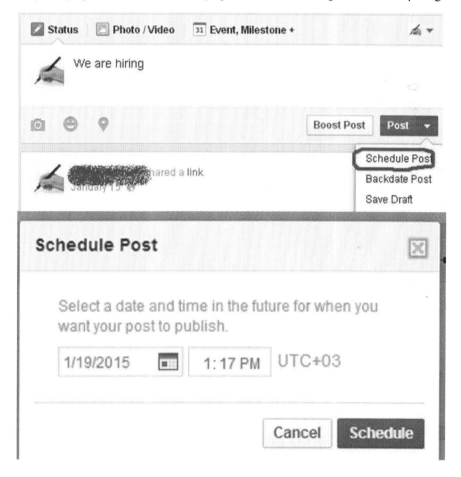

#Micro target your posts

If you are targeting specific group(s) of people with your posts, you can micro target them with ease by simply clicking on the target icon that is located at the bottom left corner then choose add targeting. You will notice that you can target your posts based on relationship status, interests, gender, language, location, age, and educational status.

#Constantly review performance insights

Don't expect to get any different results if you are constantly using the same strategies. The only way you can know how to track this performance is to check your Page Insights as often as possible just to get a clear picture of what seems to be working and what isn't working. With that, you can make sound decisions on the kind of posts to be having just to keep your page engaging and relevant. With Page Insights, you stand a better chance of understanding whatever your audience wants by simply analyzing the kind of content they seem to comment, share and like.

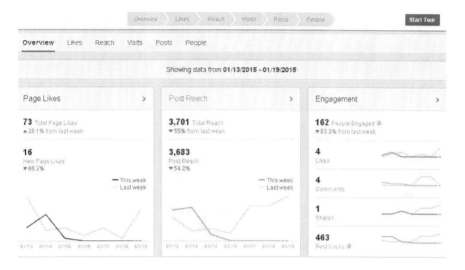

This <u>post</u> shows some advanced page customization techniques that you would probably find effective in making your site to stand out.

I had mentioned about groups in passing a while ago. Since this is a very critical part of establishing a solid foundation in Facebook, let's discuss it in greater detail.

Unleash the power of Facebook groups

If you want to develop stronger ties with your customers, a Facebook group does the trick in helping you develop and nurture strong ties. As such, you could create a Facebook group for fans to discuss literally anything. Let me explain this by giving real benefits of how this works.

#Use the group to get real customer feedback

Having a Facebook group allows you to engage with your members with greater ease especially because group updates will be visible on recent activities of different members. Since your fans cannot receive notifications about what is happening in the Fan page, a workaround for that is to have a Facebook group. This in turn enables you to talk directly to people who are really interested in the subject matter (including those who need help). Groups also provide easier engagement among members through responding to questions that members might have. Members can also post images about themselves using whatever products or services you have on sale, which in turn allows those who are still deciding to have a better idea of what to expect.

This high level of interaction enhances the truth factor between the business, customers and members, which in turn makes it easier to know what such people are interested in.

#Use a group to offer support

There will be times that customers will need help or motivation. Instead of cluttering your page with discussions (well, a page doesn't display the recent posts as a group does), you can support anyone who is in need through the group. Whether you are using an open, invite only or public group, you can be sure that a group makes it easier for some of the knowledgeable group members to assist those who need help. This in turn helps build confidence in members.

Even with a large group, it is very easy to have non-affiliated group admins to help steer conversations in the right direction.

#A Facebook group can help you to spot new opportunities

If you have a vibrant Facebook group, members will often come up with lots of ideas some of which could be very easy to implement. Even if you won't be the one to implement that idea, you will definitely find it a lot easier to sell that idea to an interested party.

#A group helps you to generate qualified leads

Members of your group have a certain interest. This makes it easier to sell anything to them with little effort while ensuring that you keep your customer acquisition costs low. Your audience (qualified leads) is equal to the number of members in your group so the more members you have, the higher the number of leads.

Before we can conclude on how to dominate Facebook, I should perhaps remind you that the more visual you are in your postings, the higher the likelihood that you will attain success. Here are some ingenuous ways through which you can become more visual in your Facebook marketing efforts.

#Convert your ideas into images

Humans are highly visual beings; we simply cannot help it but be glued to amazing images. So if you can compile everything you are thinking in some sort of image, you can easily capture the attention of your audience. This can be done through creating graphics, slideshows, images, infographics, and animations that you can use to animate and even teach your audience. You will be amazed by the high level of engagement when you use captivating images that prompt your audience to be interested. You will hardly need to tell them to share or like because they will do so without thinking!

#Tell your story

It is easy to digest information contained in an image than when it is contained in a long post. So, instead of wasting too much time writing a highly detailed story about yourself or your business, you could simply convert it to an image (some sort of a flow chart) that tells your story in a glance.

Tip: Blend images with words to increase conversions. It might be challenging for some people to understand your photo so having some words in there can help make the image clearer. You can do so with captions, photo descriptions and adding some hashtags and keywords to make such photos more descriptive.

Keep in mind that you can always hire a designer to create captivating photos to rocket fuel your campaign.

Facebook has over 1.1 billion mobile users per month and over 700 million daily users. As such, you cannot overlook mobile marketing if you really are to dominate your niche on Facebook. You need to realize that content, audience and device are not a one size fits all sort of thing; each requires a unique engagement approach if you are to dominate. So, how can you go about that? Here are some mobile marketing tips that will help you become better at it.

#Make sure that you know how your posts look like on mobile

You don't want annoy your audience by posting content that makes them have a hard time accessing. The first thing you should do is to be sure about how each post would appear if viewed on mobile. Your posts should be designed with a mobile user in mind. Such things like Facebook tabs can make your users to have an amazing or annoying experience when viewing your posts. One way of making your tabs easier to access is to custom make them using different tab creation tools.

#A mobile friendly blog does the trick

Even as you promote a website on Facebook, you cannot afford to have a site that is not mobile friendly. This is especially because a large number of mobile users will often click away if a page seems to be taking longer than usual to load. So, if you want to maximize your conversions, ensure that your blog or site loads easily on mobile.

#Geo target your audience

The fact that smartphones support GPS means that you can easily target specific groups of customers within a certain location to increase conversions. This is especially helpful in instances where you are promoting a brick and mortar business or a local event. You can combine these with click to call extensions on Google to make it a lot easier to convert such leads to paying customers.

#Listen constantly

Since your audience will definitely engage you even when you are out of your work desk, you also need to engage them constantly. You can use social monitoring apps like Mention since these often make it easy to filter sources hence making it a lot easier to engage your audience without wasting too much time.

#Don't be afraid to share photos

The good thing about social media is that it allows brands to "humanize" themselves such that the audience even forgets that they are interacting with a company; it becomes more of a personal relationship. To make your relationship even juicier, you should probably try posting photos of your business being social. These random photos really connect with your audience by capturing those "human" moments.

We will later on talk about popular mistakes that people make that make it difficult to achieve dominance status that they are always looking for; you cannot dominate any social media platform if you are constantly making some 'silly'/innocent mistakes!

How To Use Blogging To Dominate

W hat do you think of when you hear the word blogging? Well, I see blogs as information resources that enable people to make various decisions on different issues. Well, not all blogs help in decision making per se since some of them simply exist for entertainment purposes; some people want to follow the latest gossip on various people.

Before you buy any new product, you will probably search it on various search engines; the search words could be anything such as, ABC safety, ABC side effects, ABC reviews, ABC benefits, etc. From the search results, we look for such things like comments, pricing, reviews, and experiences of others with respect to that product or service. We won't go too much into detail on what a blog is and what it is not because you probably know a bit about blogging, WordPress, blogger etc; instead, we will concentrate on how to use blogs to build a strong social media brand. Here are some tips on how to guarantee success through blogging.

Know how to set up a blog

Before you can even start attracting visitors to your blog and making them click around your blog, you should probably ensure that you have set the blog properly. Whether you are using WordPress or Blogger, you should at least have some basic understanding of how to set up your blog. In essence, your blog should give users a good experience.

Optimize your blog for mobile

With the growing use of smartphones, more and more people are using such devices to access information online. So whether you are promoting your blog on social media or are simply relying on the search engines to drive traffic, you should ensure that whoever visits your blog from a mobile device has a great experience. Navigation should not be a problem. Additionally, the pages should load pretty fast. If you don't want to lose mobile customers because of a bad experience (slow loading speed or difficulty in navigation), you should probably hire someone to optimize your site for mobile view.

Get a premium domain

The blog could be part of your website for easier navigation. But ensure that it doesn't go anything like *yourblog.wordpress.com* or *yourblog. blogspot.com*. Instead, it should go like *yourblog.com*

What do you want?

Determine your objectives while ensuring that you put into consideration the way you want others to see your business. How would you want people to think about you? How can you implement that in your blog? This will help you in working around the content you publish on the blog for greater success.

Consistency pays

Be consistent in your posting. Your audience needs to feel that they can count on your predictability. As you do this, keep in mind that projects and products can come and go but your brand will remain indefinitely; your blog should be timeless.

Watch out what you post online

Whatever you put there sticks there forever. Therefore, don't put anything that could jeopardize your brand image.

Create sharable content

For every post, ensure that you have a picture to it then share that on Pinterest, Facebook, Twitter, LinkedIn, Google+, Instagram and other social networks that you could be in. You will be amazed by the limitless power of Pinterest in driving sales and conversions. People are often attracted by images; the more captivating your picture is, the more it will be shared, the more pins it will get and the more repins it gets. In simple terms, captivating photos have a high click through rate (CTR) so use them to your advantage while blogging. This should ultimately direct traffic to your site.

Get a theme color and some logos on your blog posts

People need to feel that they are visiting your blog based on the layout, color pattern, themes, and other core aspects of your blog. In essence, a logo or theme color creates a sense of brand awareness. Don't be afraid to develop a logo and theme color at the onset; actually, the earlier you start engaging your audience with all these features, the easier it will be for you to create a strong sense of brand awareness.

Develop a blogging style and language and be yourself

Your audience should be able to tell the difference between your posts and anyone else's posts based on your way of thinking, your writing style, and everything else about your blog posts. This helps in developing your brand. The point is to humanize your blog as much as possible just to make sure that your audience feels truly connected to you. You should strive to show your personality through your blogging endeavors so that your audience can truly tell who you are.

Always treat your posts as your product

In the internet, the rule goes that if you are not paying for it, someone else is. As such, you cannot afford to sell yourself short by writing blog posts that don't stand out. If you are developing a product, would you not use the best ingredients? Would you not constantly want to make it better? Before posting, be sure that people want that product (your blog post). Gone are the days when consumers didn't have an option on what they consumed. As such, you should get their input if you want to stand out from the competition. As I mentioned, if the reader is not paying the content, someone else will (is) (there is no free stuff). As such, you should always think of whether someone would actually pay for your content before hitting the publish button. Don't just give opinions on the subject; do your research if you are to stand out as an authority. That's the only way you can say that you are providing content that someone would be willing to pay for.

Give it all for free

Don't be afraid to publish content that you would actually make a living by selling. Your valuable advice is what makes you stand out as an authority. No one wants to steal your ideas. When people constantly find that you are always giving insights that they would not find elsewhere, you will be amazed by how many calls you will be getting from people who are hungry for information.

*Have a clear call to action in each of your blog posts

Always be selling but ensure that your blog posts don't sound salesy. Instead, you can have a call to action at the end of each blog post. It could be share this blog, check out our products etc.

*Guest post

Guest post in reputable blogs so that you can drive traffic to specific social media sites through leaving signatures in your posts. You should also invite guest bloggers to post something on your site. This especially works magic if you feel pressed for time. It also works well when you want to give your audience a fresh perspective; this helps in bringing in some new eyes to the blog.

*Same username

Ensure that you use the same username when creating blog posts and various social media platforms.

*Quality content

Showcase your expertise in the specific area by posting high quality informative blog posts that people will use as reference material when making various decisions or performing various tasks.

*Build trust

Work towards building trust and relationships with your readers so that they feel comfortable buying products or services from you. You cannot afford to overlook the power of personal relationships in blogging since this drives traffic to your site by making people want to check out your opinion about a certain issue of interest to them.

Consult your audience

Ask for ideas from your followers; some people have ideas about different issues but simply need someone who they consider as an expert in a certain field to address that issue. You will be amazed at how many people will be willing to share ideas on what to blog about and what kind of products or services to offer in order to make them feel more satisfied.

Inspire your readers

Readers don't just want to read about you all the time. They want to hear your perspective about different issues and how you can inspire them to achieve different goals. Readers want you to add value to their life as opposed to just entertaining them.

Make your blog easy to navigate

Don't give your audience a hard time in finding whatever content they are looking for on your site. Ensure that access to content can be done within the least number of clicks as possible.

Stop promoting on your business blog

When people are visiting your blog posts, they are not looking for unending sales pitches from one post to another. They want to interact with your company on a personal level without feeling as if they are being pushed to buy stuff; they are hungry for information so provide information that adds real value to that reader. Try to write articles/ posts that are not directly related to your product in order to provide real value to your readers and even prompt them to take action.

Strive to deal with negativity positively

The truth is that there will be people who may not like the way you think, the way you do business and everything about you. Instead of simply hitting the delete button even before you can go through all the negative comments, you should instead use these as an avenue to win your customers and even offer them guidance. You could also try to find out if anything went wrong. You should let your business have a personality then let it shine through as it deals with all negativity and adversity; you shouldn't be so scared about saying sorry!

Claim authorship for your work

Use "rel=author", which is recommended by Google to claim authorship for your work. When you claim authorship for your published articles, your profile picture will show when next to all your articles on search results on Google. Perhaps you should know that search results that have a Google+ profile picture often have a higher CTR than those that don't have.

Titles do the magic

Most of us click on blog posts because we find them descriptive of what we are looking for. In other instances, we click on them because they are catchy; we simply want to check out what the whole thing is all about. Experiment with different titles to find what works for you in capturing the attention of your target audience.

Tips On How To Use Twitter To Dominate

Twitter is the second largest social media site after Facebook with over 280 million monthly users and up to 500 million tweets sent daily. This is definitely a huge market to market your products but the challenge is; how do you do that with just 140 characters per tweet? How do you use the famous hashtags and other features that Twitter provides users to drive traffic to your blog, website or other social media sites? Here are some actionable tips to help you get the most from Twitter.

Tips on social media branding through twitter

*Know what you want

You can only know the nature of information that you will be tweeting if you know what you really want. Are you a blogger wishing to share ideas and content about what you write about or do you simply want to be sharing news or following celebrities. When you know your purpose, you will definitely be tweeting on relevant topics.

*Make the Twitter handle (name) exactly the same as your other Social Media application's page names.

*Make sure your profile has keywords

This will make it easier for people to search you on Twitter. You should also publish your Twitter handle in other platforms simply to attract a new following.

Provide all the required and relevant information while creating your Twitter account as it will make people more aware of your business.

Give your audience reason to want to follow you-Ensure that you give your audience some form of incentive of why they should follow you. For instance, you could offer exclusive access to something that your audience would be interested in. Post regular offers and promotions for stuff that your audience finds amazing.

Avoid using special characters and punctuations so that users will be able to reach your website with ease.

Customize your Twitter profile to make it more interactive and attractive. Make it look more like you. Your goal is to develop a social media brand so try to use the same branding features you have on your Facebook profile on Twitter.

Engage: Follow people or businesses that you consider important based on the industry they are in and the kind of stuff they tweet about. Go on to favorite tweets, retweet tweets, and respond to tweets. This works in that people will start listening to you when they notice that you are acknowledging or listening to them. Likewise, if anyone follows you or even mentions you on Twitter, you should try to respond to them and even thank them. Retweet any great content that you find. You will realize that more people will start engaging you when you engage them. Look for weekly chats and participate in the conversations. In this case, engage them with hashtags but ensure that you don't overuse them (one or two is just okay). Also, ensure that you don't use hashtags that could easily make your content end up being grouped with inappropriate content.

Alternate your tweeting times-The best way to know when your audience is listening is through alternating your tweeting times until you find what works for you in attracting maximum engagement.

Be creative in your content creation; use the 140 characters you have at your disposal to craft captivating tweets. In some instances, you might need to retweet other people's tweets or content unlike creating your own content. As you do that, ensure that you keep in mind why you are doing it, who is your target audience and what you hope to achieve through that.

Be captivating: Learn to use pictures to pass 1000 words as opposed to relying on the 140 characters at your disposal. Use inline images in your tweets to generate more followers. As you do that, use images that speak positively about your brand. You will notice that tweets with images have more favorites and retweets. According to the Twitter Media Blog, posts that have images attract over 30% more engagement than the standard tweets. Therefore, it is clear that you should be relentless in your image creation. Share infographics that explain some complex concepts in simple and few words. In doing so, you are bound to have far more engagement than constantly tweeting empty (with no image) tweets.

If a photo speaks 1000 words, then a video does speak 10,000 words simply because it can help "edutain" your followers and spur conversations. As I mentioned, people are very visual. Actually, a video can help you increase engagement by over 25 percent. Although photos as mentioned above have more engagement, it has been proven that videos usually have a greater effect in building relationships with followers. As such, you will find that videos can help you nurture followers until they become customers. You don't have to post a very complicated video; simply posting a photo of yourself doing something in your business could be all you need to start engagement.

As a rule of thumb, ensure that you have a clear call to action in each video then drive people to the relevant landing page on your site where whatever product or service you are selling is available. You can do all that on YouTube.

You can also hire professionals to create your videos for you.

*Consistency is key in any social media marketing effort. You can do so through creating tweets that are in line with your brand's tone, mission and vision. Ensure that your voice is unique and active on Twitter. Also, ensure that you are consistent with as far as timing for Twitter is concerned. If you are usually active on Twitter on specific days, be active on those days. You could even automate the tweeting process to ensure that you don't miss an important moment to tweet. This will make your followers expect something from you during those days, which can ultimately grow your audience.

*Take note of trending hashtags: You can ride on a trending hashtag to promote your business. For instance, you can ride on such hashtags like cybermonday, TGIF, Travel Tuesdays, Terrific Tuesdays and any other popular tags. Just check the popular tags and figure out how you can add value to the conversation while ensuring that you promote your business. Try to offer an attractive deal to get guys to like your page.

Learn to manage your Twitter account professionally. You should experiment with tweeting at different times to learn when best to engage your audience because they are listening. Also, there is a limit on the number of times you should probably tweet; you can only know that when you experiment. You could also schedule your tweets and monitor notifications to ensure that you have an organized way of doing things.

Identify influencers and work with them to grow your presence-Whether you run an online or offline business, you can seek a popular blogger within your niche then offer him or her a good deal (say a commission, discount or upfront payment) for tweeting about your business. You could then have that blogger have a unique discount code that anyone who buys from you through him or her uses to access a discount. This is a win-win for both of you because you get followers while the blogger gets to strengthen his or her following for getting good deals for his readers or followers.

Help people-If you know something that someone else might not know, don't be afraid to tweet about that. You will be amazed by the level of positive response that you will get from those who find your tweet very helpful. The rule of thumb is that you ought to treat others how you would want them to treat you if the roles were reversed. If you would sometimes want someone to help you on something, don't just withhold information that you know can help that person. Just like in blogging, don't be afraid to share it all because this will definitely pay back in multiples. For instance, if you are attending a conference, which is bound to attract people who don't live within your city, you could for instance tweet about the best hotels, best restaurants, best gyms, best cabs, best night out joints, best churches, fun things to do in your area and many other things. The more help you give, the more people feel as if they are indebted to you. Actually, they will always stop by to check out what you have been up to.

Tweet stats and data-It is very easy to click on a tweet that has figures on it than one that seems to provide an opinion on something. Giving stats simply makes you to have more credibility whatever you are tweeting about. This way, you stand a better chance of attracting people who are looking for hard facts about the subject. Stats and data have been proven to attract 17% more engagement.

Tweet quotes-Most people simply seem to like famous quotes about a certain matter of importance to them. Actually, if someone finds a quote that relates to an issue of interest, they are likely to retweet it or favorite it. A study done on 2million tweets showed that tweets containing quotes received 19% more engagement than standard tweets with no quotes.

Use the resources on Twitter to manage campaigns with greater ease. Twitter's small business planner app does the magic in getting you to plan all your campaigns, monitor engagement create a competitive edge for yourself and your business. You can find out more about the small business planner here. You can also use Tweepi or Insightpool to help you target who you should follow or who should follow you. This greatly helps you to build a network of people who have interest in whatever you are interested in, which means that your followers are more valuable than just random followers. You can as well use Twitonomy or Twtrland; Twitonomy offers analytics while Twtrland provides social intelligence. You can as well use Topsy to know whether people are interested in whatever issue you are interested in; with

Topsy, you can check the latest results hourly, weekly, 20 days, a month or lifetime.

Observe the follow-first rule and favorites follower rule-Don't be afraid to follow people. Some will be courteous enough to follow you. Also, you should favorite other people's tweets then they will probably follow you. With this option (favorite-follower rule), you can be sure of a higher quality and highly engaged following.

*Select your lists carefully-You can use Twitter lists to listen to whichever conversations you are interested in. You can also use the lists to identify influencers and even filter out any noise so that you can focus on the issues you care about.

Tips On How To Use YouTube To Dominate

YouTube is the most popular video channel with over 30 million daily visits and over 100 hours of video posted every single minute. This makes it a great avenue to establish your online brand. Nevertheless, the countless videos posted every single day onto the thousands of other videos could easily make any videos you publish end up being buried deep within the many others such that you end up not reaching out to your target audience. Just like in every other social media channel, the secret to success is getting a following or audience to broadcast your videos to. Actually, the more views you get, the more popular your videos will be and the greater success you will have in ranking highly on the search results. Here are some tips to get you started when creating and promoting your YouTube channel.

Setting up the channel and initial design: When creating your YouTube channel, ensure that you use your company's name and any relevant branding resources to ensure that your channel is easily identifiable to your target audience. Also, ensure that you have a clear, catchy and straightforward company description. Look for ways of linking your YouTube channel to your other social media pages to ensure cross promotion. You can also do cross promotion through linking your channel to other pages that you are affiliated with. When you start, the next step is to promote your channel to ensure that you get the most views to your videos. Here are some tips to get more views:

#Set up an email signature that features a link to your YouTube videos or any other videos you might have. Through that, email recipients will probably want to check out your videos. You can be changing the link when you want to promote a new video through the email signature. Also, you can post a link to your website in the description section just to drive traffic to your site. Ensure that your URL starts with http:// since this is the only way YouTube can detect that the content is a link.

#Post high quality videos that subtly attract people to click on them when they show up in the search results. In this case, you should strive to shoot and upload all your videos in HD format. As such, you must ensure that your videos are shot in an environment with very good lighting.

**Keep your videos short-*You really don't have to do hours of video to pass your message across. Actually, more people are likely to watch short videos than extremely long ones so keep that in mind when creating videos.

#Ensure your blogs have a link to your YouTube channel, as this will make it easy to attract your readers to your channel, which ultimately increases views and subscribers.

*#Have a catchy thumbnail-*To be honest, most of us only click on YouTube videos that already seem to be descriptive of what we are looking for. We mostly judge this by looking at the thumbnail. Therefore, ensure that you have one that is highly captivating to maximize clicks to your channel.

#Strive to ride on hot topics when creating titles: Although you shouldn't be misleading in your titles, using hot titles will increase your chances

of attracting an audience through organic search. This works in a similar manner with the thumbnail. A catchy thumbnail can increase the number of views on your videos to a large extent.

#Brand your videos through having a logo or channel name at the beginning of the video and at the end of the video. You could even have a video effects editor to animate your logo and anything that could make your channel even better.

#Unleash the power of annotations-You can interlink YouTube videos through annotations (these can appear at the top left and at the top right corner of each video whereby the ones at the bottom link to the previous video while the ones at the top link to the next video). You can use annotations to develop a menu screen at the end of each video whereby the viewer is presented with other videos that he or she can choose from. With this option, it will be a lot easier for people to navigate between all your videos, which in turn results to more views. Additionally, you can use annotations to point users to a playlist or the page that prompts the viewers to subscribe to your channel.

#Transcribe your videos too for SEO purposes. The content on your transcribed video will also add to the keywords, which will in turn help in driving traffic to your videos since the content is usually searchable.

#Let some background music do its thing: Don't just post silent videos (they suck!). Ensure that you have some background music for your videos just to break the boredom of watching a 2 minute video without any sound.

#Add your videos to a playlist by grouping similar videos (those with similar keywords) together in order to make better placement in the

searches. Also, search those with playlists that match your search preferences then add them to your playlist.

#Share your YouTube videos on other social media sites like Twitter and Facebook. Whenever you upload a video, share it in your networks and ask your friends to share it or like it as well. Ensure that each video has a clear call to action asking viewers to subscribe or share the videos. You can opt to use this in the middle or at the end of the video.

#Ensure that you optimize all video metadata to ensure that you drive more traffic through searches. Metadata includes annotation, thumbnail, title, description and tags. Also, ensure that the name of the raw video file is identical to the keywords you are trying to rank highly.

*#Don't overlook the power of captions-*If you don't want to lockout people who have hearing problems, you can use captions in your YouTube videos (captions are simply the YouTube's subtitles). These captions also come in handy for those who want to watch videos without turning on their volume. Additionally, the content is also searchable on YouTube's search, which in turn means you will find it easier to rank. To add captions, click edit a video then choose the captions tab.

#Ensure that you have a consistent pattern of uploading new videos to your YouTube channel. This predictability is very critical if you want to have a dedicated following.

#Ensure that you engage your followers constantly by responding to comments, suggestions and other forms of feedback from your audience. Your responses should be prompt (don't take weeks or months to respond to other people's comments!)

#Partner with bloggers within your niche: These would probably be willing to share high quality and informative videos on their blogs. With this option, you will generate more leads, more views and more subscribers. You will also have a valuable backlink to your video. Actually, having your video embedded in a page with a high page rank increases your chances of ranking highly on YouTube. You might need to give them an incentive to promote your video on their blog. You can as well have a blog that features the video.

#Be selling: You should have a clear call to action in your videos. Ask viewers what you want them to do; it could be "subscribe to my channel", "click on the link in the description", "leave a comment", "like my video", "share with friends", "add video to favorites" etc. You can present the call to action through an annotation or in person; whichever way you do it, you will notice that there will be an increase in engagement.

Tips On How To Dominate LinkedIn

L inkedIn is the third biggest social networking site after Facebook and Twitter and the #1 professional networking site with over 200 million users. This presents limitless opportunities when you establish a strong brand presence on the social media site. A strong brand presence means having as many connections as possible and engaging them actively. As you start your journey towards exerting your dominance in LinkedIn, you should perhaps keep some of the following statistics in mind because LinkedIn is different from Facebook, Twitter and any other social network:

-68%+ of users in LinkedIn are older than 35 years.

-72%+ of users in LinkedIn are college grads

-66%+ of users in Linked in earn more than $60,000 annually.

The good think about LinkedIn is that interaction is a lot more professional than in any other social site; you won't be posting photos of your recent wild parties on your profile lest your future boss sees that!

So, how can you stand out while presenting yourself professionally in LinkedIn? Here is how to get there:

#*The first step is to create a LinkedIn company page* where you will be engaging your followers by posting news, events, content and other updates. You will be amazed that having a LinkedIn page will also help you rank higher on the search engines. Research has already shown that up to 50% of the members of LinkedIn are likely to buy from the companies that usually engage them on LinkedIn.

Once you create a page, you need to optimize that page so that it can show whatever your company offers. You could even build a products and services page on your page to attract more people. Ensure that you are very convincing on why people should follow you. LinkedIn company pages are also highly SEO friendly; Google even shows a preview of up to 156 characters so you need to have a compelling description that captivates everyone. Use relevant keywords as well. Don't forget to have your company's contact information, and any other information relating to your areas of expertise in this page. After doing that, ensure that you ask your customers to endorse your products or services.

#*Complete your profile*: People want to know who they are interacting with on LinkedIn. Actually, the system is set in a way that makes it hard to find connections when you haven't filled your profile. As such, upload a good photo or logo of your company and complete every entry until your profile shows 100% complete. You can also post previous jobs or projects on the page just to show your credibility.

#*Engage your audience* as much as possible through responding to member comments. Ensure you interact with people in corporate blogs, company posts and product updates to ensure that you always keep knowledge of your company in people's minds. Also, ensure that you customize content to your customer's or follower's professional interests since this resonates with them. You can do that through sharing your content to all followers or to a specific targeted audience based on level of seniority, company size, industry or geography. Targeted engagement is a must have if you are to succeed in LinkedIn.

Always ensure that your posts start with catchy introductions and headlines; keep in mind that the audience won't read your posts if they don't find them captivating. Also, ensure that you keep your titles short (40-49 characters). Nonetheless, you can always experiment to find out what works for you. The audience determines what is interesting by a simple overview of the first two or three sentences so ensure that you start on a high note. Additionally, keep in mind that questions don't really make good or captivating titles on LinkedIn. Also, ensure that your content is of high value to your readers by ensuring that you write something easy to consume and easy to share. This in essence should include such things like pictures, chats, articles, videos etc. You could also ask questions to engage your audience more.

#Add a LinkedIn button on your website and even use it in your email and blogs signature. This should ensure that it is easy for other LinkedIn members to follow you in a single click.

#Set up a custom URL-Simply click edit profile then click edit (just besides the public profile section). After doing that, check into the right bar on an option for customizing your url.

#Send updates about job openings to your connections. Also, search and answer various questions on LinkedIn and join groups that you can participate in. You could even create your own group to discuss different issues of interest to your audience.

#Start some LinkedIn campaigns that you can use to engage your audience.

#Promote your LinkedIn page on other social media accounts to drive traffic to your page. For instance, connecting your LinkedIn profile with your Twitter account can be a good idea. One way of setting up your account for that is to auto post your tweets in your LinkedIn status. Another good way is to choose to send tweets that have #in hashtag to your LinkedIn profile. This ensures that you keep your profile clean and professional.

#Use LinkedIn publishing to grow your network: According to LinkedIn, LinkedIn users who usually consume professional content usually spend about 8 hours every week reading about industry trends and news. You can leverage on the power of LinkedIn publishing to grow an audience. You should ideally create posts that are between 1900-2000 words since this has been proven to attract more shares, views and comments. You should as well post regularly and engage your audience consistently if you really want to grow a large readership. Here are some more tips on success with LinkedIn publishing.

-Think of a middle school audience: Don't write posts that are too complicated for people to comprehend. Even if the audience is largely an educated lot, most people still want to read posts written in an easy to understand writing style. These attract more shares, views and comments.

-Don't be too opinionated: Try to jog people's minds instead of providing a good or bad opinion about an issue of interest. Back your points with data if you really want to come out as an authority in your profession.

-Use images: As I have been insisting, an image speaks 1000 words so use it to capture people's attention and attract engagement. You should ideally use 8 images to attract the maximum engagement in terms of shares, comments and views for each of your posts. Videos don't really add much value to engagement.

-Break your content into small chunks for easy reading. Don't forget to use H1, H2, H3 tags to break your posts for easy reading and improved performance. It has been proven that 5-9 headings perform better.

Tips On How To Dominate Google+

Google plus is increasingly becoming popular making it a great tool to use in order to engage your audience in a better way. Here are some tips to help you solidify your brand on Google+.

#Optimize your Google+ profile for search while ensuring that it is captivating to your audience. Your brand color and logo should be in the profile and any other stuff that you want your business to be identified with. As I already mentioned, it is best to use a profile that is consistent across different social networks.

#Use Hangout to thank or praise certain groups of customers, as this provides direct face-to-face interaction between customers and businesses. You can get valuable insight on how to enhance customer experience through Hangouts.

#Give your customers or audience an opportunity to participate in the business process. You could blend this with allowing your audience to see the human aspect of your business. Hosting a Hangout is actually one of the easiest ways through which you can make customers have that kind of experience due to the face-to-face interaction.

#Promote your content on Google+ and ensure that you use Google+ as part of your email signature. Always ensure that you give users an option to + your content by adding a Google+ icon on your blog posts. This is referred to as Google+ badge. As I already mentioned, cross promotion will be an asset in driving your social media brand to success.

#Participate in Google+ communities in order to drive traffic to your profile; Google+ communities are just like Facebook groups. You should combine this with using Ripples to determine the effect of different marketing techniques in enhancing your brand image.

#Use images and videos to captivate the target audience; they say a picture speaks 1000 words so use this to your advantage. The more you captivate anyone who sees your posts, the bigger the following you will receive.

Tips On How To Dominate Instagram

With over 200 million active users, Instagram stands to be a great tool for you to tap into the immense potential that the platform offers in generating leads and increasing conversions. However, before you can jump right into Instagram, you should probably understand that you won't have the luxury of publishing links to your eCommerce site, pushing sales, and pumping products through countless advertorial copies. You can only stand out based on how you set up contests, how your profile looks like, and how you create your photos. So, how can you stand out from the competition?

#Create a killer Instagram profile

Let me explain how you can achieve that:

-Use high resolution photos-These are likely to grab the attention of potential buyers with a lot of ease. If you want to stand out from everyone else who is using smartphones to capture photos, get a good camera or hire a pro to take high resolution photos.

-If you are selling something, ensure that you make it absolutely easy for people to buy. You can do this through posting an image description to include a link to the specific page where that product can be purchased. This can greatly maximize conversions.

-Avoid hard selling on Instagram-You can probably post photos that feature what people can do with your products or services. This subtle selling strategy greatly helps connect with the audience, which ultimately results to increased engagement and conversions. You can greatly boost your company's reputation by posting in-the moment photos that make your audience feel more connected to your business.

-Nurture the habit of using Instagram Direct. This service enables users to send messages to specific users. You can target your recipients based on their location and demographics. This means greater engagement and higher conversions. Since it has been proven that the most active fans are the ones who convert more, you can simply find who is most active then send them messages introducing new products or introduce giveaways (promotions) and even run contests. You can also use this option to drive traffic to your website.

-You can as well post offers and discounts on your profile to increase engagement and visits. Since people love free stuff, they will be very much willing to visit your profile very often if they are assured that they might get free stuff. You can also blend this with regular giveaways and contests to keep people coming back to your page. As you do this, ensure that you use a special hashtag especially one that has your brand name in order to attract engagement.

#Try streaming your Instagram photos on your website. This greatly helps in building awareness about your brand. As your audience grows, you can start generating buzz about your brand through private and public campaigns, contests, and giveaways. So, what kind of contests can you have?

>Like to win contests-You simply need to ask users to like an update after which they will be enrolled in the contest to stand a chance to win. These are very easy to enter, easy to set up and easy to use to grow an audience. However, these have low engagement and low consumer engagement.

>Hashtag user generated contest-simply set up a hashtag for your contest then ask users to post a photo or video then use the contest's hashtag to participate. This helps strengthen your connection with the audience and helps popularize your brand especially if the hashtag has your brand name in it. However, this increases barrier to entry because you are asking users to generate their own content.

>Email gated contests: In this case, you ask people to provide their email addresses to participate in the contest. This makes this an excellent option for building a mailing list.

#Use text overlays on your images

Communicate any information you want to pass across to your audience through text overlays. You can use any photo editing software to achieve this.

#Have clear calls to action in your captions

Don't be vague on what you want your audience to do. Ensure that you are very descriptive of what you want the audience to do. You can have such calls to actions such as "like it to lower the price"; in this case, you should set milestones of how many likes you should get to lower the price by a certain percentage. You can use others like "click on the link in the bio section".

#Unleash the power of hashtags

Your captions or comments should have relevant hashtags to help you increase your reach, overall visibility and engagement. You can use hashtags that are related to your business, your target audience, your post and anything else. Unlike in Twitter, don't be afraid to use many hashtags (as many as 30 hashtags or more). Try to incorporate a mixture of popular, unique (custom hashtags) and less popular hashtags. 5-10 hashtags are often the best though.

#Use other social media platforms

Cross-promotion can greatly help you increase your audience. You can cross promote your social media accounts just to increase your audience in each platform.

#Be unique

Your uniqueness or creativity in your photo creation will ultimately determine whether your photo stands out or not. You can showcase your talent in cooking, dancing and doing lots of other things. DIY how to videos can also do some magic in impressing your audience and generating a larger audience. You should also ensure that you bring out your personality excellently such that your audience can clearly tell between your content and other people's content. You shouldn't forget to post consistently though; this helps you to build trust.

#Unleash the power of analytics to determine your performance. Such analytic tools include Iconosquare and Totems. You should also have your benchmarks like the number of likes, comments and shares based on the number of your followers. Additionally, you should try posting at different times to know when you get the most engagement.

Tips On How To Dominate Pinterest

If visual marketing is the current trend coupled with the fact that a picture can tell 1000 words, all you need is Pinterest to tell your stories. As you have noticed throughout the book, I have been emphasizing on the importance of using pictures, videos and other visual stuff to captivate your audience. Actually, research shows that Pinterest brings in more buyers than any other social media site, ahead of Facebook, Twitter and Google+. So, how do you succeed on Pinterest? Here are some tips to guide you towards success:

#Ensure all your blog posts have a captivating photo so that you can share it on Pinterest. If you have older posts that have no photos, start adding photos on them then pin them.

#When creating an account, ensure that you create a business account so that you can benefit from the many features that Pinterest has tailored for businesses. It also gives your brand a face that people can associate with. If you already have some followers on a personal account, change it to a business account. As you do this, ensure that you use a profile image that people can recognize easily; it could be a logo or a product that you want to be known for.

#Partner with influential guest pinners in order to help drive new interest to your boards. This can ultimately drive sales and following, which ultimately increases brand awareness.

#Be creative in the way you engage your audience (followers). You could show them that you appreciate by baking a cake for them and pinning the photo on your board. You could also find a way of ensuring that you inspire your audience based on the kind of pins you have. You could also use this to help people generate new ideas on various aspects of their life. This should help you in getting more pins, followers and repins.

#Ensure that your bio and board are fully descriptive. Categorize your pins so that anyone can navigate your page with ease. However, ensure that you don't have too many boards that could end up having irrelevant photos.

#Be a regular pinner. This can be a great way of attracting a huge following by engaging them actively since very many of your competitors might probably not be pinning regularly. This means that you can easily attract a fairly good following by just pinning as often as once a week. With regular pinning, you will be creating a competitive edge.

#Don't just focus on pinning photos. You can start pinning videos on YouTube and Vimeo, which means that you can easily cross promote your channels through this visual board.

#Follow more people on Pinterest and be a regular pinner and repinner. You should also ensure that you engage your followers by thanking those who share or repin your pins. Thank them by repinning their content as well. The more you do that, the more you will have an army of people who will be constantly pinning, sharing and following your content.

#Have a board where you pin your products and product ideas. Also, ensure that you have a Pin it button on your website, blog posts, and other places. This should make it easy for your followers to pin and follow you.

#Show the human aspect of your page by sharing your goals, preferences, style and aspirations. In a bid to do that, you could have a board about whatever happens behind the curtains (who is behind the business, how do you do stuff etc). People like knowing stuff about others.

NOTE:

Ultimately, always ensure that you check out what your competitors are doing on their social media accounts; you could get a lot of insight on how to mold your business for the best.

Don't Make These Mistakes If You Want To Dominate Social Media

#Being narrow minded in content creation-You should create content in different topics, use multimedia and create content that is well researched to add value to your audience.

#Overlooking the importance of analytics-You cannot know how well you are doing unless you measure performance. As a rule of thumb, the numbers never lie; your gut feeling could be very wrong.

#Assuming that one technique fits all. Different platforms are different. Don't just push content and ideas to them. Understand what they want then develop a strategy for providing what they want not what you are selling.

#Being overly self centered-Don't just talk about yourself all the time. You should share user generated content and even curate content.

#Failing to promote your content after creating it-Different social networks work well for different types of content. Know which works best for the particular type of content that you are sharing. You should also post evergreen content and partner with influential people to promote your content.

Conclusion

Thank you again for downloading this book!

I hope this book has helped you learn about some effective strategies and techniques you can use to create a strong social media brand presence.

Finally, if you enjoyed this book, please share your thoughts and post a review on Amazon.

Thank you and good luck!

Free Bonus Video: How To Create a Social Media Marketing Strategy

Jim Tobin, president of Ignite Social Media, shares the Ignite Method of Social Media Marketing Strategy Development. The company has developed social media strategy for some of the world's largest brands and this 25-minute presentation outlines their process in detail.

Bonus Video: https://www.youtube.com/watch?v=dCJv4rmWdMA

Made in the USA
Lexington, KY
27 August 2015